To

_____

From

_____

Date

_____

A RoseKidz® Rhyming Book

Precious Blessings: What Is Church?

RoseKidz® is an imprint of
Rose Publishing, LLC
P.O. Box 3473
Peabody, Massachusetts 01961-3473 USA
www.hendricksonrose.com

Cover design by Chad Thompson
Illustrations by Chad Thompson
Interior design by Drew McCall

ISBN: 978-1-62862-783-1
Rosekidz ® Reorder # L50022
JUVENILE NONFICTION/Religious/Christian/Devotional & Prayer

Printed in China
Printed October 2018

What Is Church?

Valerie Marie Carpenter

 HENDRICKSON PUBLISHERS  ROSE KiDZ

A Meeting Place

I love to go to church. Do you?

It is a meeting place

Where all God's children come

And gather in one space.

All the believers were together.

Acts 2:44

4

It's where we worship Jesus.

He is the one true King.

It's where we pray and
learn God's truth.

It's where we praise
and sing!

Worshiping God Together

6

Praise God in his holy temple.

Psalm 150:1

7

Celebrating the Good News!

It is not that we loved God. It is that he loved us and sent his Son.
1 John 4:10

It's where we celebrate the news

That Jesus came to save,

And all of those who trust him

Receive the love he gave!

9

All God's Believers

Did you know that church is more

Than just a place you go?

All God's children are his church

From now and long ago.

I will be their God. And

they will be my people.

Ezekiel 37:27

A Family

The church is all of God's people,

Not something built by hands.

The church is one big family

Gathered across the lands.

You are also members
of God's family.
Ephesians 2:19

A Place to Do Our Part

Like different parts of a body

That all do different things,

The church's members
are given gifts

To glorify their King.

You are the body of Christ.

Each one of you is a part of it.

I Corinthians 12:27

God-Given Purpose

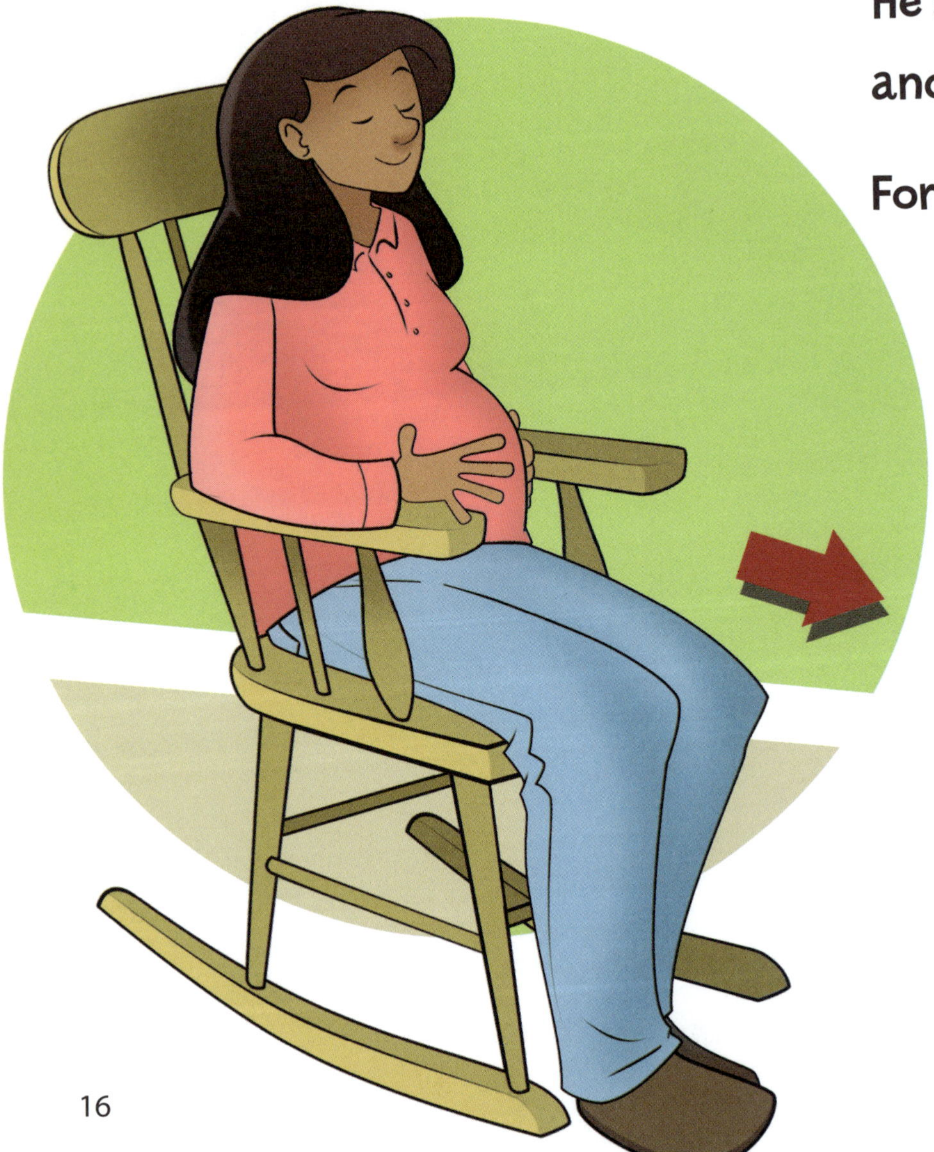

God has given all his people

A job to do on Earth.

He's had a plan
and a purpose

For you before your birth!

Before you were born I set you apart to serve me.

Jeremiah 1:5

Serving Others

We'll serve in many different ways

With our hearts full of delight.

No matter what it is we do

We are followers of Christ.

18

So eat and drink and do everything else for the glory of God.
I Corinthians 10:31

19

Encouraging Others

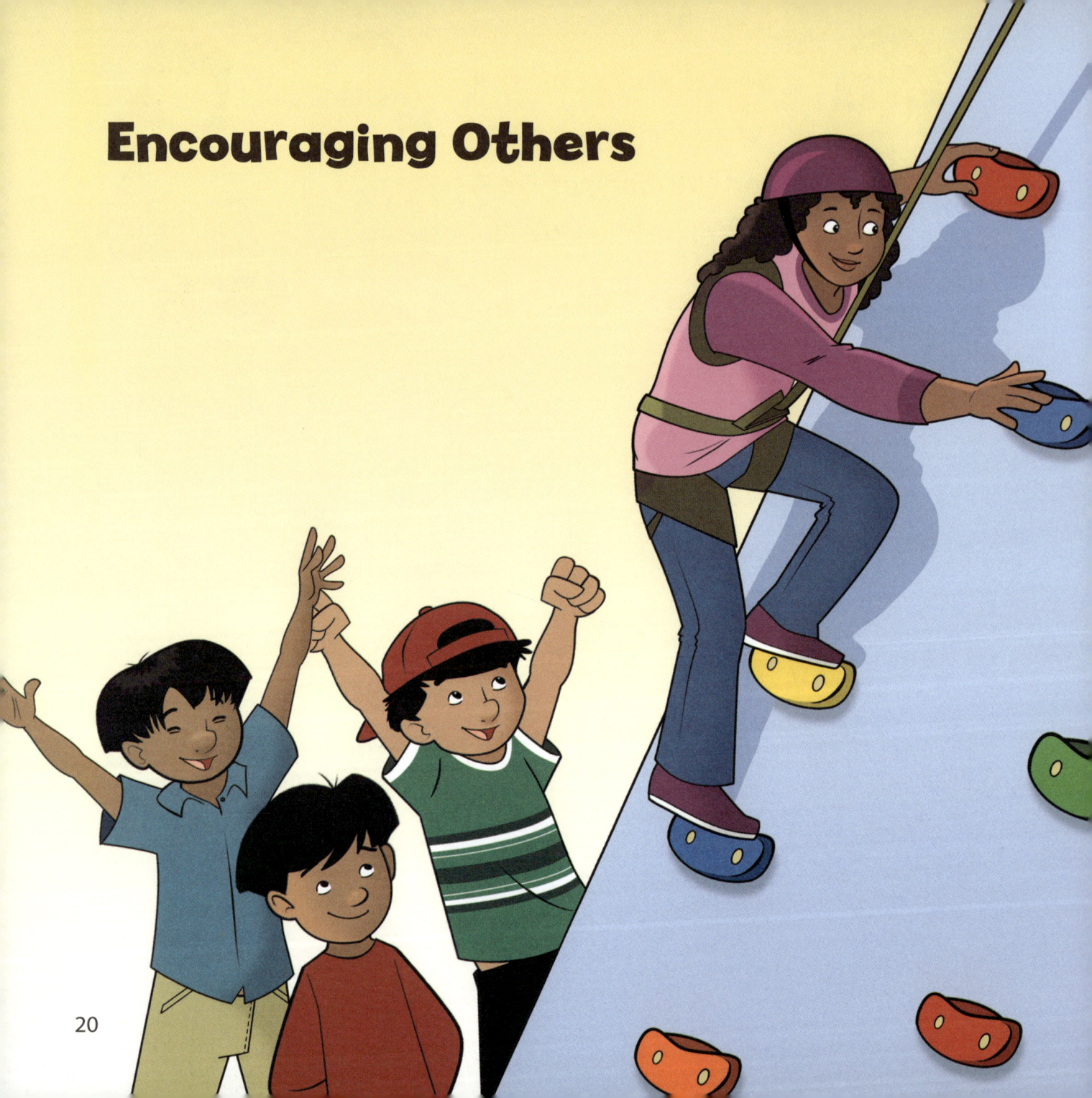

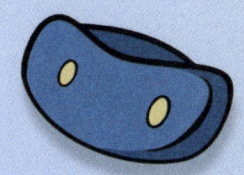

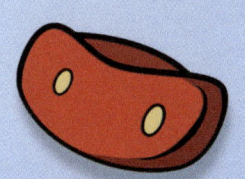

We're called to build each other up

With our deeds and with our words,

Encouraging one another

To love and do good works.

Let us consider how we can stir
up one another to love.
Hebrews 10:24

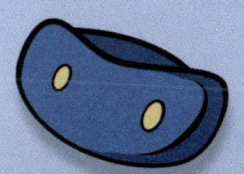

Loving Our Neighbors

We are called to love our neighbors,

Our sisters and our brothers.

The world will know we follow God

When we love each other.

If you love one another, everyone will know you are my disciples.
John 13:35

The church is like a bright city

Sitting on a hilltop,

Shining to far-off places,

God's light that never stops.

You are the light of
the world.
Matthew 5:14

God-Given Life

And this is the light we carry:

The message of God's love.

Anyone who believes in him

Gets life from God above.

Anyone who believes in [Jesus] will
not die but will have eternal life.
John 3:16

27

Sharing the Good News with the World

God gave his church a mission

To share and spread good news!

So go make followers of Jesus.

You really cannot lose!

You must go and make disciples of all nations.
Matthew 28:19

Where You Belong

The next time that you go to church

Remember all along,

You're part of God's BIG family,

And it's where you belong.

God chose you to
be his people.
1 Peter 2:9